THE INFINITE SPARK *of* BEING

—— The Agreement ——

BALBOA.
PRESS
A DIVISION OF HAY HOUSE

Balboa Press books may be ordered through booksellers or by contacting:

Balboa Press
A Division of Hay House
1663 Liberty Drive
Bloomington, IN 47403
www.balboapress.com
1 (877) 407-4847

Print information available on the last page.

ISBN: 978-1-5043-9371-3 (sc)
ISBN: 978-1-5043-9373-7 (hc)
ISBN: 978-1-5043-9372-0 (e)

Library of Congress Control Number: 2017919265

Balboa Press rev. date: 03/07/2018

To all of my Teachers,
my life is the gift of your lessons.
Though at times I am a poor
representative of your teachings
may this book be a benefit to all.

PREFACE

The name The Infinite Spark of Being refers to the interconnectedness of all living beings that is a constant thread throughout Buddhism, Hinduism and various other traditions. In the Bhagavad Gita Lord Krishna tells Arjuna, "All living entities are My part and parcels." Later Krishna also states, "He who is rooted in oneness realizes that I am in every being; wherever he goes, he remains in me."

Who Krishna is or what God represents, is not the point. I myself understand this to mean that we are all part and parcel of the source from which we are all being spun.

Through various practices these verses and ideas went from being concepts that I had simply accepted, and only knew intellectually through trust in the teachers as well as the dharma, to being undeniable truths that I knew inwardly. They became more than ideas. They are now in the fibers of my being. They are deep in my marrow. The name The Infinite Spark of Being is to serve as a reminder that you and I have lived millions of lives. We have been brother, sister, mother, father and lover to every single person that we lay eyes on. I loved them once before, and I need to continue doing so. That was, and still is, my work here on this plain. To become more compassionate and understanding.

This book is a collection of writings and illustrations. The writings are reportings of what I have found to be true and what I have experienced through meditation and other practices. However, I can only report on these things from where I sit at this point along my path up the mountain. The illustrations are made up of symbols. Most of these symbols have come out of meditation sessions over the last six years. In these sessions some of the symbols would come with a phrase or an idea. I have always felt a compulsion to record them and share them.

In the beginning I felt that it was coming out of my subconscious, and since I was artistically inclined this was how my brain was presenting the information to me. For instance if I say the word "cat" to you, you will picture a cat in your mind. So for me when the phrase "Begin to remember yourself." came through and was accompanied by a symbol and a composition.

If we can quiet down and listen to the more subtle vibrations in our life then we can receive signals or clues as to what the next skillful action might be. Today I see these symbols as a collaboration. I hesitate to say I am being given anything. I do however believe that our ability to inwardly grasp certain things can be enhanced by becoming inwardly still. Once we become quiet our mind will dress the information in the costume that we understand best.

My hope is that this book serves to remind us that we are far more than what they said we were. It is not that they lied to us. It is just that they are scared. I would like this book to turn your mind toward a higher reality. The reality that you are wild and infinite. The reality that you, the real you, was never born and you will never die.

YOU ARE ALREADY EVERYTHING
The Society for The Infinite Spark *of* Being

THE CALL UP THE MOUNTAIN

Friends,
We are all going up the same mountain.
It is the fog of the ego that tells you otherwise.

So climb.

See your perspective broaden.
See the paths up the mountain mingle and merge.

This ridge, though it seems high, is not the peak.
It is your ego that tells you that you have
summited.

Look up friends.
There's more.

As you ascend this long winding road enjoy.
Because these harsh inclines are purposeful.
These uneven paths are purposeful.
Your pain is purposeful.
You are purposeful.

I've slid down at times and forgotten the view.
Taken different paths to get back to those vistas
once savored.

It's all part of this journey we're on.
We all go up the mountain eventually.
Even those adverse to heights and wilderness
will have to climb one day.
Sure you can hide down in the town for a while,
but eventually the mountain calls you,
and you will answer.

WE'RE ALL GOING UP THE SAME MOUNTAIN
The Society for The Infinite Spark *of* Being

THESE DAYS

These days it is apparent to me that we do not belong in their city.
We belong under blue skies and the wise hammocks of the oldest oak trees.
We belong together on the open road with the radio so load that the speakers buzz.

We should go seek that ribbon of highway that Woody talked about.
I'll bet it's beautiful.

I've never seen the Northern Lights.
I've never been to Yellowstone,
and I've never climbed the Grand Canyon.
However, I have seen you sleep,
and I have kissed your face a million times,
and I will kiss your face a million more.

We live in interesting times you and I.
I do not feel attached to it anymore.
So let them tear it down.
You and I will stay in bed with the Truth
and find Its warm feet beneath the covers.

HOW THIS WORKS
The Society for The Infinite Spark *of* Being

THE AGREEMENT

They stood out there on the edge of everything looking down.

"Are you ready?" She asked with a soft smile her hand holding his.
Their fingers loosely intertwined.

"Yeah." He sighed. "You know I hate this."

"I know you do but it's how it works. Ya know?" She reminded him sweetly. She knows this always hurts him more than it hurts her.

"It just takes so long." He said his voice was nearly a whisper. He stood there nostrils flared as he alternated between chewing he cheek and biting his bottom lip. Nervous, eyes squinting deep in thought.

"But you always find me don't you?" She mustered a reassuring smile giving his fingers a small tug. Their hands hanging there together. Their fingers bent and twisted holding one another.

"I do." He muttered as he continued to abuse his bottom lip staring out at the white glare of nothing.
"God it takes so fucking long." He added as his fingers twisting tighter around her's.

"Yeah. Sometimes it does. Then other times it doesn't. What about that one time?" She reminded him excitedly.

"Yeah, the one time. And the rest? What about those?" He reminded her only turning to look at her for a moment then back out into the nothing.

He was so tired. His chest hurt to think about it how long it takes to find her.
She is always so strong and so brave. She does it for him. She has to hold him up at times like this. God knows he holds her up when he finally finds her. Everything he does is for her. The books, the songs, the poetry. It's all for her. Every birth he finds her and makes some grand statement of love to her. Sometimes it's met with a teary eyed hug. Other times a shrug of her soft cruel shoulders.

"We have to go." She reminded him. Her fingers slowly releasing his.

His hands hung heavy at his sides as he stared off into that familiar expanse of white light.
His head shook softly in disgust for the pain he was now feeling. He knew that the only way to shut it off was to step out into the suffering with her.
As she stepped out into the nothingness he followed. His eyes closed tightly. He tried to recall all of her faces he had known. Flipping through them like old photos until it became harder and harder to remember her. Until she was only an urge, a feeling. Something he forgot but knew he needed to remember.

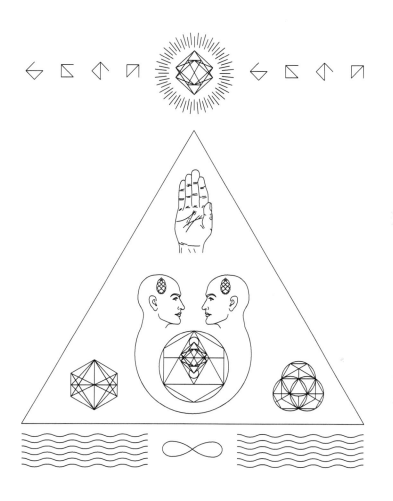

THERE ARE OTHER PLAINS
The Society for The Infinite Spark *of* Being

FINALLY WILD

Of course we all want to leave.

We all believed that we were
destine for greater things.

And maybe we all still are?
But are those "great" things measured by
men that place their treasures where moth
and rust doth corrupt
as it said in the book of Matthew?

I'm not comfortable with their
system of measurement.

My spirit requires more than they can give.

It's not need.
It's a requirement that fills me.

Water is a requirement.
Vitamins are a requirement.
Candy is a need.

They deal in candy.
Not in nutrient rich sustenance.

How can we be expected to
live on their hollow calories
of material want?

That's fine for them,
but you and I
we need more.

Their cities are boring and plastic
and these peoples' hollow dull eyes
lack the sincere nature that
feeds good conversation about
meaningful things.

Let's leave.

Let's get out from under their
toiling grind.

Let's finally run wild.

BEGIN TO REMEMBER YOUR *SELF*
The Society for The Infinite Spark *of* Being

11

A GOOD LIFE'S SLEEP

We will do this again I promise.
Don't be so afraid.
Just be here with it for now,
and know there will be others.

One evening you will wake up into the
daylight of your next dream.

The relief of a good life's sleep.

BUILDING UPON OUR CURRENT UNDERSTANDING
The Society for The Infinite Spark *of* Being

THERE IS A VALLEY

There is a windy valley of tall grass that is lit by the moon.
And there is a soft white light that washes over everything.

I run smiling.
I am alone but there is someone else here.
I can not see them, but I know that they are with me.

Is that you? Is that you the name that was given to me
by the woman? She said that your name was Edgar.

There is an ocean in the distance.
Also lit by the soft white light of a full moon.
There are tall structures that I feel
house souls that I cannot find the details of.
I just know that they are there.
They have windows that glow with yellow light.
Like candles.

I run wildly through the field at the bottom of this valley.

Is this were you live?

I am wearing a heavy sweater.
                                    Though I don't wear sweaters.
My hair is shaggy and long.
It is blond from the sun.
I see myself as a teenager.
though my face isn't so clear,
but I know that it is me.
The feeling of my adolescents
radiates from me.

I am the one running and I am the one watching.

The sound of wind and rustling grass.
The sound of the ocean.
My feet crunching the ground beneath me.
I wear heavy brown pants and brown leather shoes.

The air is filled with laughter,
but not the sound of laughter.
It is the feeling of laughter.

Edgar, we need to talk.
This place is beautiful.
Why didn't you show me sooner?

When the wheels of the body turn the doors will open.

THERE IS SOMETHING ELSE HERE
The Society for The Infinite Spark *of* Being

IT'S HARD TO SAY

The brilliance.
How they came.
Disguised as imagination.

GATEWAY MESSENGERS
The Society for The Infinite Spark *of* Being

GOD AND CONSCIOUSNESS

The Soul is part and parcel of "God".
God is consciousness.

Consciousness is in a constant state of creation
and always becoming.

God in constant play. Creating Itself over and over again.
Discovering Itself since time immemorial.

God evolving amongst Itself.
Consciousness evolving through being.
Beings, the result of Consciousness.

Life, a result of conscious creation

Ego is the result of evolution. Competition creates ego.
The ego needs defense.

Ego is primal. Ego is God loosing Itself.

God is never lost. God never forgets.
God is playing the game with Itself.

Everything is conscious. Nothing is unconscious.

All particles are consciously creating.
Multiplying.

Form is the result of Consciousness.

Compassion is the realization of the truth of reality.
The realization that It is Itself.
The realization that It is looking at Itself.

The Soul springs from the One Consciousness.

The Soul is in love and when It sees Itself
for the first time It is not lost.

There is only One Consciousness
and it wonders far from itself.
It will eventually come home.
To God meeting God.

A return to God. Coming home to the Divine Mind
and leaving once again.

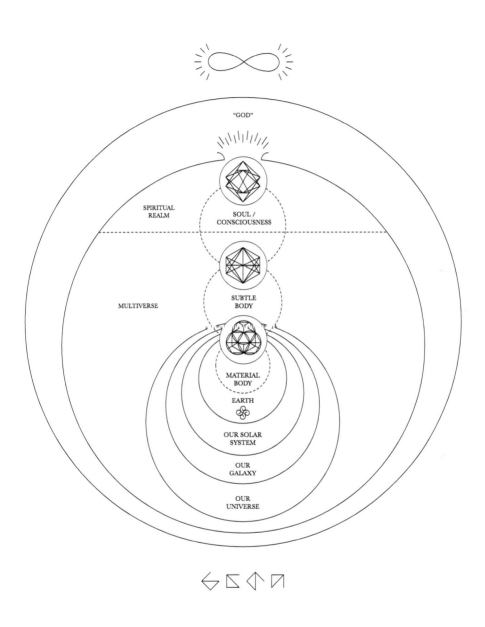

"GOD"

SPIRITUAL
REALM

SOUL /
CONSCIOUSNESS

MULTIVERSE

SUBTLE
BODY

MATERIAL
BODY

EARTH

OUR SOLAR
SYSTEM

OUR
GALAXY

OUR
UNIVERSE

SOURCE DIAGRAM
The Society for The Infinite Spark *of* Being

EVEN THE GUY IN THE HAT

I imagined that they were all rays
of the supreme conscious raining down.

"Even that guy in the hat?"

Some times that thought comes to me
and it hurts. It makes me sad
and I don't even know why.

But last night it was the funniest thing
I had ever heard of.
Watching us all wonder lost through a grocery store
pretending we didn't know one another.

Acting like we weren't divine beings of light

Sometimes that separation is needed
and becomes the path back to You.

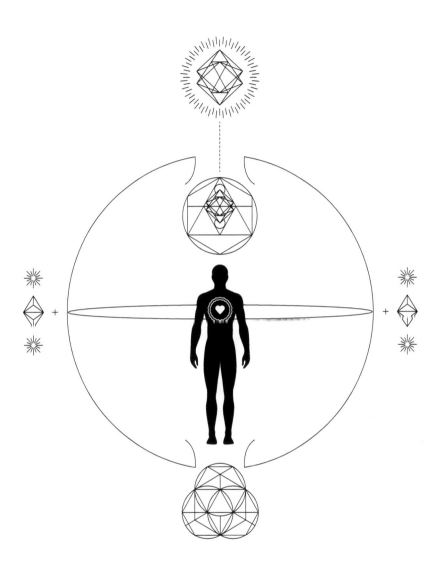

HEART FIELD
The Society for The Infinite Spark *of* Being

CAPTAINS BOUND TO ONE ANOTHER

There was never an exact moment
that our souls met,
and there will never be an exact moment
that they are separated.

We are bound to one another
through the divine consciousness
that is constantly in creation.

Creatively at play with itself.
God constantly finding itself,
losing itself, and the entire time
falling in love with this dance
over and over again.

We have to learn to watch our lives unfold.
To see the perfection of the past
and not obsess over it.

"The wake does not steer the ship"
Allan Watts once said.

You can see where you've been
but don't try to navigate your course
by using your past.

Leave it there
where it belongs.

ONCE WE ENTER THE STREAM
The Society for The Infinite Spark *of* Being

23

THE LAST CLINGING

There are moments that I feel an ecstatic bliss towards the idea
of one day shedding this body and moving on.

Then I think of you.

I think of your eyes,
your smile.

Then I feel fear.

I feel that clinging and grasping to life.

I've tried to figure out what I would need
in order to give up the ghost quietly.

I would need you to promise me that you will come and find me again.
To promise me that we would do this again only sooner in the next life.

We waited so long this time.

I know our incarnations weren't ready,
but god damn it, it felt like a lifetime.

It was always so hard with the others.
But you, you make it so easy.
You love me just the way I am.
Where I am.
You demand nothing from me but
an honest and open heart.

Watching these thoughts I see the patterns.
I see that I am clinging to these feelings of love.

I try to quiet myself and remember that
this grasping is only happening on this plain.
Once broken free, my consciousness will purify
and I will realize that we cannot be separated.

If I could only stay quiet.

It's so depressing.
All of this spiritual practice and
I'm still attached to you and your love.

Your flawless
and unconditional
love.

AND SO WE BECOME FEARLESS
The Society for The Infinite Spark *of* Being

IT ALL GOES ON WITHOUT YOU

What if death was the gift?
The goal.
What if we were meant to die?

Of course we die our bodily death.
So in a way we are meant to die,
but what if we understood that we were
meant to die?

Could we then shed the anxiety
of leaving behind the ones we love?
Would the knowing that this life carries
on without us become easier to welcome?

I know I will die.

Lately I feel an urgency to things.
I sense the past.

My ego begins to speak to
time being wasted.

Quickly,
I reign the ego
and remember the infinite moment.
I remember that this is the mind.

This experience is the mind.

YOU WERE NEVER BORN
AND YOU WILL NEVER DIE
The Society for The Infinite Spark *of* Being

THE BREATH OF THE EGO

The mind is the lens through which we interpret the world.
The ego is the hot breath of fear that fogs the glass.

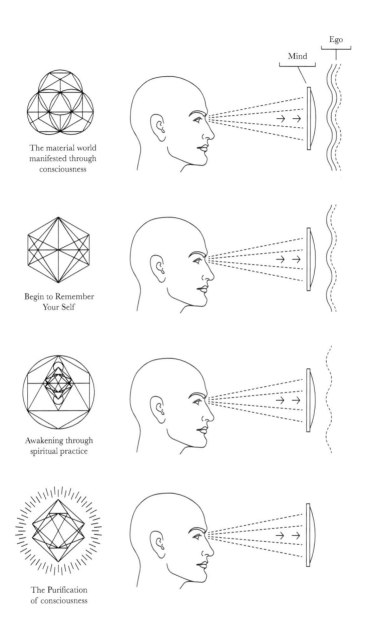

The material world
manifested through
consciousness

Begin to Remember
Your Self

Awakening through
spiritual practice

The Purification
of consciousness

Mind

Ego

→ →

EGO *AND* MIND
The Society for The Infinite Spark *of* Being

LET GO LIGHTLY

I felt so open.

It was probably a combination of a few things.
But when I walked down the street every person I saw
was a person that I knew. Someone that I had loved.
Maybe not in this life but probably in the past.

It felt like my chest was a giant hole.
It was filling with love for everyone and everything.
It was like I couldn't hold all of it but I wanted to try.

Well it's happening again.

And like before it's probably a combination of a few things.
Like they say a leaf falling at the right moment could wake you.

I don't try to hold onto it anymore or try to re-create it when it fades.
I just let it pass through me.

I try to let it all pass through me.

I see where I cling. I remember where I stick and I let it all go.

"Let go lightly" I heard him say.

It's a powerful dream, this life. It hurts.
But for those moments where it all falls into place,
we go on.

Love. Family.
The way it feels to laugh.
The freedom of a good cry.

For me even a funeral
has a comfortable softness to it.

But don't chase these mystical experiences
or feelings of light.
They are meant to be rungs on a ladder.
And like most things they will change.
They will disappear.

They aren't meant to stay.
They are meant to be teachers.
They show us what is possible,
and give us hope that
we can find our way home.

AS THIS VEHICLE BEGINS TO ASCEND
The Society for The Infinite Spark *of* Being

31

THOUGH ROUGH AND WORN

You have always out grown things handed down to you. Haven't you?
It is a wardrobe of clothes that never quite fit.
Their bad taste and crooked seams were never quite what you wanted.

The sleeves are always too short.
Your shoulders are always too broad.
The yoke of their shirts aren't made for someone like you.
You can carry the world on your shoulders.
Don't they understand?

Their clothes are confining,
and these thin soft threads won't ever hold you in place.
Your mind is too wild to be fulfilled by ideas that aren't your's.

Let your heart run wild.
Let it run naked through this plain.
Purify your mind till nothing can hold it.

See clearly.
Your eyes are not blind folded with their cheap ideas.
Your's is a free life. A loving life.

Over time you found things that fit you.
Sometimes a patch work of ideas.
A non-linear way of being in this world that works for you.
You were never going to fit in their shoes anyway.
Why start now?

Your feet, though rough and worn,
they are your own.

PASSING THROUGH THE GATELESS GATE
The Society for The Infinite Spark *of* Being

A PLACE I'VE COME TO FORGET

I drove south hard along a highway deep in the woods. At the time I was telepathically communicating with my deceased father. I was telling him that there had to be a place between West Palm Beach, Florida and Miami, Florida that he would like.

"There is a place. It has marshlands and hills." I told him through telepathic vibration. My hands at 10 and 2 on the wheel.

The thought of this place came into my mind very clearly though I did not know where it was or how to find it. It was more of a sudden thought form than a direction. At the same time I could see my father's image clearly in my mind. He was smiling at me over his shoulder in a white T shirt.

I had set off alone leaving my girlfriend, in some sort of market place to waste time while I searched.

For what I do not know. I did know that we could not go back because there was no "back" to go to. As I drove I saw a river to my right. I wouldn't call it a raging rapid but it was certainly a swift moving river.

Some rivers barely move. Their current is slow. Those rivers, to me, seem dirty and stagnant. The kind of water that if you were to swim in it, it would make your skin feel slippery and itch. This rive I saw was not like that at all. It was clear and deep.

Behind the river were hills. Tall for hills but certainly not mountains. All topped with tall pines. They weren't Florida pines. They were Northern Pines in assemblages varying in sizes. Though a strange sight to see in this part of the country, I was given to the feeling that it was more of a special place than an anomaly.

I pulled off the road in awe and walked with amazement down a slope. There were people wandering around the area. All older than I. They felt quiet and meditative. I noticed that some were emerging from a wooded area that resembled a trail head. I assumed that it was a trail head because of the official signage posted at the parting of trees. Completely over taken by the beauty I did not read a single sign. Looking around I began to wander about the area and down the path against the flow of people headed in the opposite direction.

This place was beautiful. The grass was lush and green. The trees were tall in their clusters. Thick green branches hung heavy from trunks who's bark had a red hue.

Meandering down the wide path, my head on a swivel, I came upon a wooden building. It was tall with stairs leading in and out. It resembled an enormous tree fort. As I approached I was given the sensation that this was a communal living area.

I entered curiously. There were stairs along the wall. I ascended a set to the right leading to walkways that lined the inside of the building spiraling upward. Along these walkways were open doors leading to the rooms where healers lived. There was nothing indicating that these people were healers other than a vibratory sense of their purpose. This was their home. I hesitate to say they couldn't leave, but they couldn't. However, it was more out of purpose than anything sinister. They were all similar in appearance. Grey hair, male, glasses, white linen shorts and no shirt.

I walked along peeking, from the corner of my eye, into each room until the wall curved giving me a better view into one room at the end of a long track of open doors.

There was a healer sitting in a tall wooden chair. Tall in that it sat higher then the average seat. The healer, a man, had chin length grey hair that was slightly wavy. He wore small round glasses. They were more like spectacles that sat lower on the bridge of his rather large nose. Below his nose was a thick grey mustache that hid his upper lip and a portion of his lower lip. His arms seemed long. He was thin but pot bellied. He sat shirtless in his white linen shorts over a white haired elderly woman. Her hair was short and curly. She was very grandmotherly, a bit plump wearing a navy blue shirt with little red flowers and red trim on the neck and sleeves as well as navy blue polyester slacks. I do not recall her footwear.

She sat below him with her back turned, hunched over in a smaller wooden chair. The healer was bent over her pressing his forearm against her back in a massaging circular motion. He looked up as I approached. Lifting his forearm from the woman's back he sat up and leaned back into his large wooden chair. His eyes never left me. The woman sat up, gathered her things, and left as if I had just arrived for my appointment with this healer.

I walked into the room as if it belonged to me. The healer stood up and watched me closely. He was tall. He never smiled. He never spoke and neither did I. Entering the room I looked around. It was a small space. To the left was his chair. The legs were tall and the back was broad and high. The smaller chair for those being healed sat in front. Next to his seat was a wooden desk. It also had a smaller wooden chair with it though pushed in underneath. To the right was a closet with the doors pulled shut and an alcove where his small wooden bed was pushed against the wall. The head at the far wall facing the door. Straight back, across from the doorway, was a wall with only a window. It looked out to those tall hills and Northern Pines. I walked toward it and looked out in disbelief. It didn't look like anything I had seen before. As I looked out I could feel a warmth in my chest. I felt a sense of belonging. It was like I had just come home. My mouth slightly open. I wanted to speak but all I could do was smile. I turned and looked at the healer. He was smiling warmly. Saying nothing he nodded goodbye as I left the room.

As I left I felt accompanied by something. It was an awareness. It had no body. It was just aware of me and I it. I descended a few flights of stairs and exited a different door than I had enter. It was on the left.

I walked out onto a deck of a crystal blue lake surrounded by trees and hills. It was connected somehow to the River I had seen earlier.

There were people standing around looking out at the beauty around us. Some were in small groups talking quietly amongst themselves.

"I have to show this place to someone. Someone has to see this." I thought to myself.

I walked looking for the way out. The entire time scanning for landmarks. There was a fear of not being able to get back to this place. I could see my car up by the highway as I emerged at the trail head. I kept turning around looking behind me frantic that I wouldn't remember how to find this place again. As obvious as it was to see from the road there was an impermanence to it the hung over me. Each tree, each rise and fall of the earth, like a cartographer, were cataloged in my memory in hopes of using them to get back here.

At the top of the slope I stood with my hand on the door handle of my car taking one last look around. My father came to mind.

With a full heart I drove north back in the direction that I came from. I was trying to hold the experience in my mind. Trying to recall my steps so that I could return, but as I drove the memory of this place drifted farther and farther into the back of my mind. It began to dissolve slowly from my memory until it became a faint recollection of dream I once had about a beautiful place. I could feel my heart breaking. I felt a deep longing for this place. Was it like the rest? The visions of places from past lives that I still had a longing for? I felt connected to them still. Was this just like the others?

I drove with a faith. The faith that, while this place was incredible, my path was not to cross with those trees and that river just yet.

Exhaling I rested at the bottom of my breath and let the warmth wash over me. Smiling softly I let it all go.

AS BEAUTY BECOMES MEANINGLESS

I can't even look at the sun now
without thinking of you.

Every star, every cloud,
every beautiful thing I see
means nothing to me if you are not here.

What is that?
That thing that makes the world
less important without you?

Come and find me
when we leave this place.
When we wake from this dream.
I am sure that I will still be in love with you.

THE CHURCH OF WHAT WE HAVE FOUND
The Society for The Infinite Spark *of* Being

LET THEM STAY WITH YOU TONIGHT

Greater than the pain of love lost
or the death of a loved one
is the realization that everything you want
is only the acculturated response
to what they wanted you to feel.
And what they want you to feel
will always serve their interests.

Brothers and Sisters, please see clearly.
The mind is the lens. The ego is the fog.

Don't let them scare you into buying their fears.
Those fears are dead weight.
Those fears are boring.

Live with an open heart.
Assume the best in people.
Be free.
It is the ego the separates you.

They want you to live in their cages.
They want you controlled.
The wind off of your wings
rattles the cages that they have built for themselves.

These are cages of the mind. The cages of thought,
of storyline run wild.
These bars are made of ego and are meant
to defend the fragile sense of self, of identity.

As for you, you are nothing.
You are nothing in the same way that there
is nothing in a clear blue sky but vast beauty.
You are nothing in the same way
that there is nothing on a new canvas
except pure potentiality. Ready to become beautiful.

Let them fill themselves with things that break.
Things that become useless.
Let them have everything that makes them feel whole.

It is a harder path that they've chosen.

They're good people. Just scared people,
and there is no crime in being scared.

We have all earned shelter tonight.

WE ARE BOTH EACH OTHER
The Society for The Infinite Spark *of* Being

I CAN'T GO BACK TO SLEEP

I can't go back to sleep
if sleep means forgetting
what we've done here.

I was 5.
Things were different.

That is when we start to forget.
That is when we forget who we are.

That was when I forgot.

However, I have become quiet.
At times I remember villages
where we all live together.
There is a closeness, but I do not know why.
It is always after something that has shifted.
Like the earth itself changed.

These are happy times.

It is a feeling that we are staying behind
to work on something.
It's not hard work.
It's just a feeling of necessity.
It feels light.
It feels effortless,
but it must be done.

THROUGH THE CROWN
The Society for The Infinite Spark *of* Being

KARMA / PERCEPTION AND EXPLANATION

If you can quiet your mind enough to experience your perceptions as the Witness then you can see your karma actively unfolding. Your preferences will dictate your perception.
The Third Patriarch of Zen states, "The Great Way is easy for those without preference." Though we all have our preferences that come with being a human we do not need to be attached to those preferences.
So we learn to notice them without becoming attached to them.

In the example you see 2 beholders and 1 event. Both beholders are entering the same event. See the beholders with a lens.
Each patterned differently by past experiences.

Notice how the patterns of past experiences change the perception of the event for each beholder. You and I, as outsiders, see the event as it is, but when the 2 beholders view the event, through their respective lenses, the views are not what you and I see.

These preferences are one aspect your karma. So by being attached to a particular pattern, view point or experience, that gives you an unfavorable view of a particular event, you are experiencing "bad" karma. If you are not attached to your patterns (past experiences) then you improve your karma.

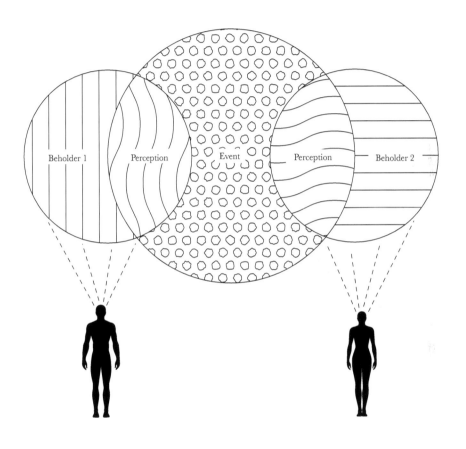

KARMA / PERCEPTION
The Society for The Infinite Spark *of* Being

THE MYSTICAL EXPERIENCE

Would you like to change your consciousness?
Would you like to have mystical experiences?

Then find an unobstructed view
of a sunset.
Stare up at the clouds.
Jump into an angry sea.
Sit and stare into her eyes.
Find somewhere outside of town
where you can see the stars. Then stare up at them
until they move. Then realize they are staring back at you.

There is knowing and then there is Knowing.
There is the intellectual knowledge that
there is something more happening here.
Then there is the inward Knowing.
When it becomes part of your biology,
when it is so deep inside of you that to
deny it seems laughable.

But always be careful.
This is also a trap.
It will separate you from everyone you care about,
but only for a time. Because the pendulum has to swing
to both sides before it can settle in the middle.

The sun will go down.
The clouds will disappear.
The ocean will calm itself.
She will leave.
And the sun will come up.

Even awakening can lead to sleep.

ONCE STUDY BEGINS
The Society for The Infinite Spark *of* Being

OUR HOME STATE

As kids we drove till the sun came up in Ohio.
Those days we were so young.
Kids in jeans and dirty t-shirts.

There's something about being on the road
with friends that feels so lonely at times.

But when you get those moments
when you can drive alone
the world is your friend.
Every car is filled with
the ones you've loved.

I don't think that could happen with you.
I don't think I could ever feel alone with you.

Watching the highway unfold
with you at my side.
Your cross stitch.
My audio books.
Our fascination with the tree lines
of our home state.

I love you.

UNTIL I FIND YOU AGAIN
The Society for The Infinite Spark *of* Being

"THAT'S MY GUY"

My family was always very open about death. It was never a subject that we shied away from.
Every time there was a death in the family my Mother would take me to the viewing.
To some people that might seem very peculiar. And at the time I thought it was just a big pain in
the ass. She was teaching me something though. She was teaching me about the thing that most
folks ignore or pretend cannot happen to them.

Often she would allude to the fact that the body was a shell.
That it was a vessel that carried your soul.
I guess by taking me to these wakes and these funerals
it was her way of showing me that it really was just a shell.

On one weekend when I drove down to visit my parents. My Father was downstairs messing around
with his antique cars and what not. Even as he was going for chemotherapy and radiation therapy
he never stopped working on projects. He would spend most of his day under the house working on
cars and things. He told me one time that he would rather die standing up than die laying down.
Even though he could see that his life was coming to an end he stayed proud and strong as long as
he could. Mostly for our benefit I imagine.

It was late in the afternoon.
I and a few others, family members mostly, were sitting around the dining room table at my parents
home. My Mother was milling around the kitchen. My Father was dying in the next room.
He had been diagnosed with cancer five years prior and at one point was diagnosed cancer free,
but as my Father would say, "Life, no one gets out alive".
During his illness and decline I often found myself more concerned with how this was going to
affect my Mother. Let's face it none of this would be his problem once he passed. I would see the
struggle that she was dealing with and thought to myself how she would be able to get her life back
together once he died. So out loud I said,
"You know, once Dad passes you will be able to heal and move on."
To think of what I said now makes my stomach hurt.
My Mother looked and me and said, "I would take care of him in that state
for the rest of my life if I could. That's my guy."
At that point I realized that, that was my Mom's love.
At one point they were boyfriend and girlfriend.
That was who she fell in love with.
That was probably the first time I saw my parents as two kids that fell in love.

I will be 40 years old next month. As time passes I see how extraordinary my parents' marriage was.
It puts her loss in perspective. There was my Mom, walking my Dad home as he stood at the edge
of the mystery.
All of mankind's biggest questions about to be revealed.
And there she was. Watching him go. He would move on and she would be left behind
to heal and to try and hold what was left together.

My Mom still sees my Dad.
She sees him standing out on the porch looking at the water.

"I miss your Dad's mind the most." She says.
"He always knew what to do."

48

AN OPENING GATE
The Society for The Infinite Spark *of* Being

I HAVE SEEN LIGHTS

I've seen lights and colors.
Images that emerge from the patterns
and speak a language that echoes in my chest.

They come and go passing through my field of vision.

My body gone.
My mind on fire.

The roar of silence
like a warm blanket.

"If I can find the tunnel
I can find my Self."

The purple path up the spine
to   f r e e d o m.

There are days that feel like loss.
When there is no peace of mind.

Those brisk walks in the woods feel like
a dream come and gone.

"Where did I go?"

I sit thoughtless
in the hottest fire.
Burning alive.
Barely conscious.

"Wake up!"

Breath slow.
Close your eyes.
Roll them back up toward the brow.

Now find the tunnel,
and find your way home.

AFTER THIS COMES LOVE AND REST
The Society for The Infinite Spark *of* Being

YOU ARE WILD AND INFINITE

Turn off your television.
Open your windows.
Find open spaces.
Run to the ocean.

"The sea will speak to you
if you become quiet enough."

There is magic in these mountains.
There are spirits in these old tall pines.
These are the places they wrote about.
The places they sang for and explored.
These are the places that notions arise from
when the wind howls.

Brothers and Sisters,
you are wild and infinite.
You are the wolves and the fish.
You are these trees and these rivers.

So when you sit, sit like a mountain.

None of these places will last.
These buildings will fail.
These trees will fall.
And these mountains?
Even the mountains will change.

So go easy Brothers and Sisters.
Be kind.

It is a long walk home.

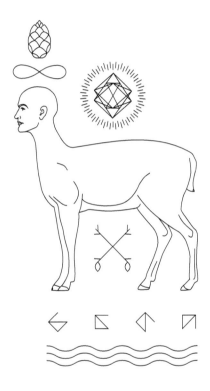

YOU ARE WILD AND INFINITE
The Society for The Infinite Spark *of* Being

THE GREATNESS OF AMERICA

The greatness of America
does not lie in its ability to kill.
But rather in the hearts
and minds
of its citizens.

It lies in the brilliant ideas
and ingenuity of the average man and woman.
It lies within the ideas
that feed families
and opens doors for strangers.

The greatness of America
will never stand on the backs
of those who are broken
and hunched over.

The greatness of America
is found in the warm hug
of those who will never
be willing to let others starve
and die alone.

Do not worry about your history.
Let go of your cultural identity.
It's spotty at best.
Concern yourself with today.

The willingness to share
is the greatness of America.

It will never lie in the
green hands that strangle
single mothers and desperate fathers.

Your wealth will not define this country.

America will be defined
by love.

CLEARLY CONSTRUCTED
The Society for The Infinite Spark *of* Being

FONDNESS FOR THE PROCESS

Sitting quietly in the warmth of darkness, while resting at the bottom of an exhale,
I began to have the recollection that I had in fact died many times.
It wasn't that I was seeing each death, but instead it was a deep knowing that there we so many.
My intellectual knowing became sincere and internal. I held the deaths as one object in my
consciousness.

After several minutes there was a rush. A wave of comfort. My eyes teared up.
There was sweetness. There was a feeling of fondness for this process.
Then came the recollection of many births that also had a sweetness to it as well.
Though birth is the beginning of so much suffering there was a pleasure to it.
A smirk and a nod to the pain of the human experience.

NEVER FORGET THAT THERE IS A PROCESS
The Society for The Infinite Spark *of* Being

A FIERY KILN

There is an unbelievability to life
once the veil parts
and you see things
as they are.

There is a certain amount of fear and trepidation
that drops away with experience, wisdom
and the inward Knowing.

Once I saw a room where beings
made of white light stood congregating.
All with a sense of amazement.
There was love and greeting.
All awash with the same sense of awe.

We've done this so many times you and I.
Over and over.
Love then death then congregation
before the thrust of unfinished work is continued.

The human birth is the kiln where the soul
cooks it's karma.
Cooking it over and over again until
it all becomes ash
and there is nothing left to burn.

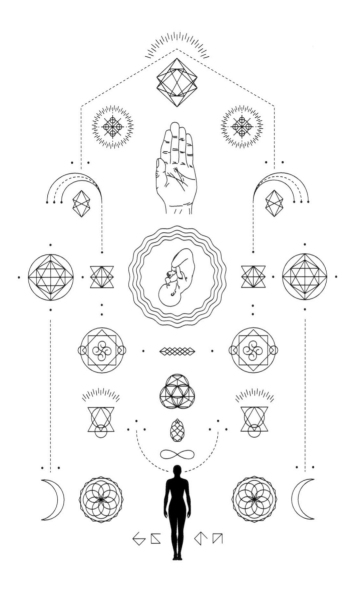

PORTAL
The Society for The Infinite Spark *of* Being

BUT WHATEVER YOU DO DON'T GO BACK TO SLEEP

There is no going back to sleep
now that we are awake.

We will lose our minds if we try.

I am in love now with the lightness.

Your world is so heavy.
I can't bear to hold it up anymore,
and pretend that it is all that you say it is
when I know it is nothing but
a projection of your own fears.

I can't live in your fear.
I don't even understand it
and I can't pretend to.

I have my own fears to deal with.
I have my own struggles with sleep
to tend to.

The struggle to stay wide awake
in the face to these lullabies is
fierce at times.

These sweet distractions singing
me back into slumber.

Rolling back and forth like a toddler.
Fighting the urge to close my eyes
and fall from that ladder.
You know, the rungs I left behind?

I guess that's ok too.
It's all part of the dream right?
Falling asleep and waking up several times
in the same night.

This night.
This realm.
This version of earth.

It's hard but I'll just keep
getting quieter and quieter
until the silence becomes
so loud that it keeps me awake.

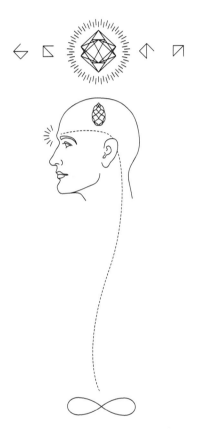

WHEN WE FOLLOW THE SILVER THREAD
The Society for The Infinite Spark *of* Being

YOU WERE RIGHT

You were right.
I finally found you.

Though I would see your face
in visions from time to time,
this agreement is hard on me still.
I don't know why we do it this way.
Why we choose to suffer over
the freedom of the astral plain,
over an expanded consciousness
and boundless awareness.

Why can't I forget you?

I'm doomed to long for you with every birth.
To chase you until I catch you.
And when I do…

bliss.

DID YOU FIND WHAT YOU WERE LOOKING FOR
The Society for The Infinite Spark *of* Being

THE WISE ADVICE

The warmth of the darkness becomes illuminated.

Starting with purple,
then yellow,
then a brilliant white light.

I feel that darkness around me like a warm blanket
that holds me quietly.
The settled feeling that allows you to rest there.

Purple lightening flashes through my head
behind me eyes.

These visions don't have the weight they once did.
I don't cling to the experiences like I once did.

They are causal phenomena
and hold no substance for me anymore.

"Teacher, when I sit I can see all of the Buddhas.
All of the Dakinis. It is so clear!"

"Don't worry it will all go away.
Just keep practicing"

NEVER BE AFRAID TO ASK THE ONES WHO KNOW
The Society for The Infinite Spark *of* Being

THE SCARF AND THE DOVE

We've been doing this for so long you and I.
We've been each other's mother, father, sister, brother.
You've made me laugh till I couldn't breathe,
and I've made you cry till your body ached.
We forgot haven't we?
We were spun from unity into this separateness.
Into this ego where we are fearful and frightened.
Grasping and pulling. Holding and clinging.
Hanging our past like a weight from our necks.
Our minds never rest. Always filled with nonsense and worry.
The concern of things we can do nothing about and things that no longer exist.
I'm sorry I hurt you. I'm sorry I took you away from your family
and those that needed you most. I gained nothing from it.
I'm also sorry I lied to you those times we were married.
The way I hurt you. I was wrong, but my ego was so powerful. I was blind.
I wish I could remember the times you asked me to marry you.
How I took your hand and the times that you took mine,
what it was like and how happy we were.
Our children and our families. God we were married so many times.
Probably as many times as we killed one another don't you think?
I wish I could remember the lessons I taught you when you were my child.
Or the lessons you taught me when I was your's.
I could use those wise words now for myself. I'm so foolish sometimes.
These bad habits are hard to shake you know?
If I can't remember what happened when this incarnation was only three years old
then how can I possibly hope to remember a love that happened
hundreds of thousands of years ago?
I think I'm finally starting to wake up. At least I hope I am.
I'm so tired. These incarnations are so exhausting, and they seem to go on forever.
When I first realized that I was working towards leaving this behind,
and getting off this wheel, I felt sad.
All these things we do. The beauty of life. How amazing it all is.
But the more still I became the more aware I became.
The more aware I became the more awakened I was.
I started to see this all as a distraction.
I started to long for understanding, but if longing and desire are hooks
then even this longing for understanding would lead to suffering, anxiety
and disappointment.
It is all a trap.
As one wise old man said,
"It's all a trap, but you have to become trapped for the trap to work."
So gladly I step wide eyed and faithful into ritual and practice.
Sitting longer and more quiet every day.
Feeling the changes in my heart and in my mind.
The opening up. The widening. The beautiful space
and the full potentiality of emptiness.

IN THE BEGINING
The Society for The Infinite Spark *of* Being

ONCE I NEEDED YOU

Once I needed You.
More than once in fact.

Once I needed to know that
You would be there if I fell apart.

I found so much comfort in believing
that You were holding it all together.
All I needed was to get closer to You.

Then I realized that I am You.

Your grace is the quieting of my own mind.
There is an understanding that lives
in the center of the chest.
The size of a thumb.

Glowing golden light.

It is all of the wisdom,
all of the creation.

Sit.

Be with that Knowing.

And know that you are that.

THEY'VE GATHERED AROUND YOU
The Society for The Infinite Spark *of* Being

FREEDOM IS FREE

But freedom is free.
It is the birthrate of all men and women.

However, one is born into the control of a system, and
within these systems freedoms are legislated away.

These systems are made up of men and women, and
their identity relies on their position within the system.

When one's mind is attached to their identity
self-preservation takes hold, and anything
that challenges that identity will be seen as a threat.

There is a need within these systems to remain relevant
to the people under their control.

Power is causal.
Power requires an object
of control.

Do what you want.
Just know that they will fight to defend their identity should
you question the role of the system within your own life.

They need you to need them.
Don't ever forget that.

You don't need a master. You need a clear mind
free of fear.

You don't need a boss. You need an open heart,
a full heart.

We will never play their game as well as they do
and that's ok.
We know the truth of life, and the nature of reality.
We've listened to those that went further up the mountain,
and they were right.

It's gorgeous up here.

THERE ARE STORIES THAT WE TELL
The Society for The Infinite Spark *of* Being

MY FATHER NEVER DIED HE JUST CHANGED

I've always felt more like I was watching this body rather than being this body.
Teachers have always talked about cultivating that witness.
I never felt like I had to cultivate anything.
It was always just there. Watching this vessel grow and change.
How its mind developed and what it clings to.

I remember being a kid and staring into the mirror, and thinking how strange it was that I felt like it was something I was wearing and not something that I was. I feel like the idea of the "vessel" made the most sense to me when my father died. After he passed and my mother, cousin, aunt and family friend left the room I stayed behind.
I pulled up a chair and held his hand. It wasn't as weird as I thought it was going to be. After all he was my Dad.

I realized this was the very last time I would ever see his form. It was like something was telling me to sit there and just be in it. It wasn't stressful or heavy. In fact the room felt very light. As I sat there it all changed. What I saw as my father became a shell. It was like I no longer identified this body as "father". The sensation of "father" felt like it was not leaving but moving. Redirecting itself. I let go of his hand and left the room. The next time I saw the body it was draped over a large man's shoulder, wrapped in a white sheet and being carried down the stairs to a white van. It was a bit strange to watch I'll admit. I was standing next to his father watching this. It was a surreal day. Immediately the house felt different. I can only speak for myself of course, but the air didn't weigh as much. The disease was gone. Or maybe it was my own selfish nature that was relieved to not have to deal with a father that was dying and all jarring activities of the day that come with that. Is it wrong to want him to pass on so that we can all begin putting things back together? Of course I'm asking because a piece of me feels guilty, but is that guilt my own acculturation? That tiny piece of me that still associates "father" with physical form?

A few of us had various experiences, sensations and sightings.
The only thing I've had were a few dreams.
I recall one dream being very casual. We talked, chuckled. It almost had this air of "Well damn ain't this some shit?" Then we parted ways. It was like we just said, "See ya later." No big deal just going the other way for a while. I woke up teary eyed and smiling. It was good. It was nice.

There was another time I dreamed of him.
I was in a church sitting in a pew. It was the second pew to the front. He walked up and just smiled. He didn't say anything, but there was energy flowing from him. It was very beautiful.
I woke up with a big smile on my face and began to cry a hard elated sob.

I still get a little chocked up at times. Usually when I hear Warren Zevon's song from his last recording called Keep Me in Your Heart for a While.
One time I heard Ram Dass say that you are done grieving when you realize that the love you shared with that person is a part of everything you do. Like it is just a part of everything. Maybe to say that they are now a part of the love you have for the family that is still living? Whatever the case I feel like I am so close to fully embracing that now.
I have never felt closer to my Dad than I do now.

There is no death.
Just difference.

72

STAY BRAVE YOU WILL BE FINE
The Society for The Infinite Spark *of* Being

MORE ADVICE ON MYSTICAL EXPERIENCES

I have a solution to your desire for mysticism.
Listen to Jimmy Hendrix's All Along The Watchtower
with your eyes closed through headphones.

If that does not induce an altered state of consciousness try
Jefferson Airplane's Don't You Want Somebody to Love.

THIS IS ALSO SOUND
The Society for The Infinite Spark *of* Being

WHERE WE LEFT OFF

Where did we go?
I could have sworn we were right here.

Everything has gone white.

"Now let's breathe deep
and see where this leads us."

I can't remember your hair
or the veins in your hands.
Or what your voice would sounded like
when you would wake me up as I fell asleep.

I love you.
I know that.
I've always known that.

I can see the coming and going of all of this.
I can hear the voices that passed through us.

I love you.
Where you lead me.
I love you where you left me.

THEY LAID THE PATH BEFORE YOU
The Society for The Infinite Spark *of* Being

NO LOSS. ONLY CHANGE.

There is no loss.
There is only change.

That is the most difficult lesson to learn.
To see things as change and not loss.

Nothing can last.
It all has to go away.
We are all going to go away.

Everyone you love will die.
Everything you own will be lost.

The glass is already broken friends.

At some point your practice will go from
self improvement to learning how to die.
Because your death will be the most
important day of your life on earth.

You are going to die.
The shoes will come off.
The lines will be cut
and you...

you will be fine.

NO LOSS ONLY CHANGE
The Society for The Infinite Spark *of* Being

CHIN UP

Warm, black,
purple pathways.

I can feel the energy in my arms
leaving through my fingers.

I can see the edge of the white light over my head.

"Edgar is that you?
It's been months since we've talked.
It's been days since I've sat here."

This exhale warms me.
Resting at the bottom of the breath warms me.

And that breath dissolves every fear I have.

Pulling the universe down into my chest
my fingers drag through stars like
bioluminescent ocean water at night.
I pull my spine straight.
My head hanging from a string.

It's so simple.
Don't complicate the practice
with your goals.

Be alone.
Be quiet.

Change will come outside of the experiences
of color and imagination.
These are only meant to lead you further
down the rabbit hole.
Treat them like rungs on a ladder.

The real change will happen
at traffic lights and four-way stops.

The real change is taking the call
from your mother, and sitting through
the questions and stories
that you've heard a thousand times
with gratitude.

So chin up.
Stay the course.

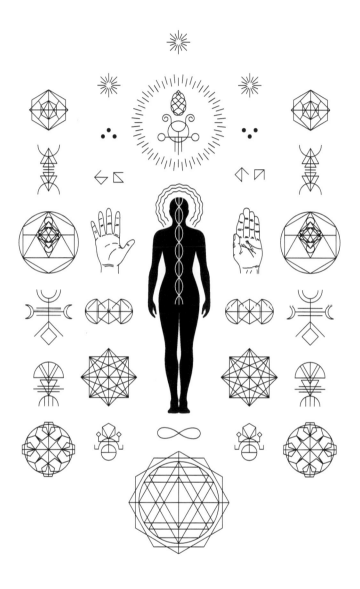

TO AWAKEN THROUGH THE BODY
The Society for The Infinite Spark *of* Being

WHEN I DRIVE WEST

When I drive west and watch the oranges and pinks
of a setting sun funnel down between the tree lines
that tower over the edges of a two lane highway,
I wonder if our fondness for sunsets and sunrises are all because
we are reminded of the place from which we are spun?

Does it remind us of the pallet belonging to
those realms of color and light?
Those brilliant plains we've passed through
on our way up through the crown?
Are those the soft colors of true freedom?
Not the legislated freedoms that are gifted to us
by a controlling class, but the freedom of being
a bodiless celestial at home in the realms between worlds.

There are times I have remembered.

I can see the tunnels.
I still feel them flying beside me.
Beings of radiant light that guide us through these realms.
They feel like love.
They feel like beautiful music.
A soft glowing hum that fills my ears.

We remember these places.

Somewhere in the deepest parts of our bodies
there is a recording of the past.
It reminds us that we have lived before.
Always returning to this plain
to recapture a piece of this experience.
Just one more love.
Just one more first kiss.
Just one more time can we please have that
first accidental touch that opens our hearts?

Finding one another over and over again.
All of us in love.
Always returning.
One moment more beautiful than the last.
None more precious than another.
We are all adored here,
and we are all in love.

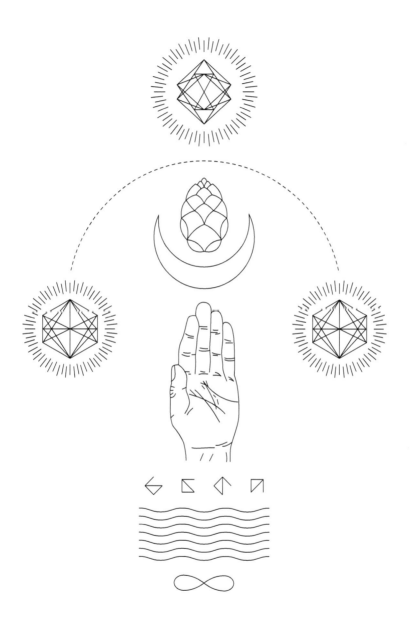

REMEMBER
The Society for The Infinite Spark *of* Being

IF THE LESSON

When my soul found itself ready to take birth, once
again, it was consigned to the lives of the two, in
which it had made an agreement with.

As this body has matured
the soul has lead it through its curriculum.

It has a spiritually restless karma, this soul.

Always wanting to free itself from this realm.
Always finding the appropriate teacher for each
lesson. It has taken each course fully.

And now it finds itself here.
Drawn to you.
Its path leading into your's.

The lanterns you've lit,
It follows each.

If this lesson is love
you are the teacher.

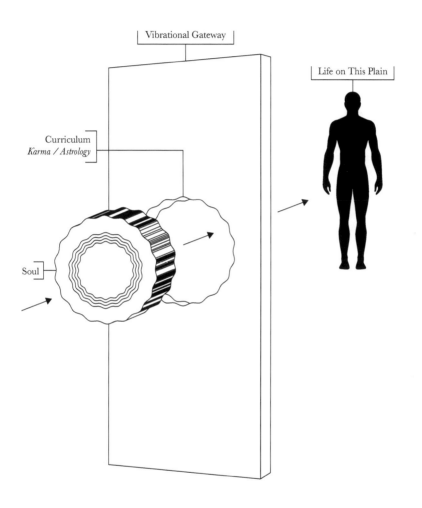

Vibrational Gateway

Life on This Plain

Curriculum
Karma / Astrology

Soul

HAVING TAKEN BIRTH
The Society for The Infinite Spark *of* Being

FULL AND EMPTY

The truth about your essential nature
will never fit into your wallet.
It will not fit on your feet nor
will it lay comfortably over your shoulders,
and make you more appealing others.
You know what you are.
You know why you're here.
You've just forgotten.
There are some for whom
"The dust is thin".
They are here to remind us that
we are not what they say we are.

We all have the same mind
and the same Clear Light Nature.
We are at our purest form empty.
Empty like a fresh sheet of white paper is empty.
Empty like a new canvas is empty yet full of possibilities.

Full of pure potentiality.
Full in its emptiness.

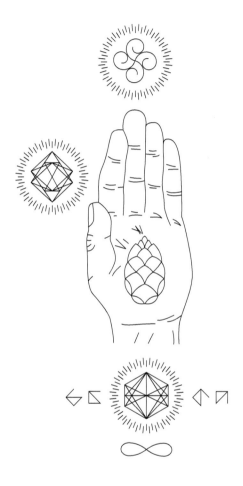

WE AWAKEN BECAUSE THIS IS NOT ENOUGH
The Society for The Infinite Spark *of* Being

WATCHER OF MYSELF WATCHING MYSELF

Breathing slow
I will rest at the bottom of each
breath in hopes of finding you
over and over again.

I will let the warmth wash over me.
I will not be a hero and struggle.

Breath will always happen
With or without my mind the breath
is always happening.

There is no need to do anything.

We are always doing something.
We cloud our vision with goals and
achievements until the simple act
of sitting still is pushed completely
from our minds.

I found you there.
I will continue to meet you there.
Behind the silence
where I watch myself
watching myself
as the watcher
of my Self.

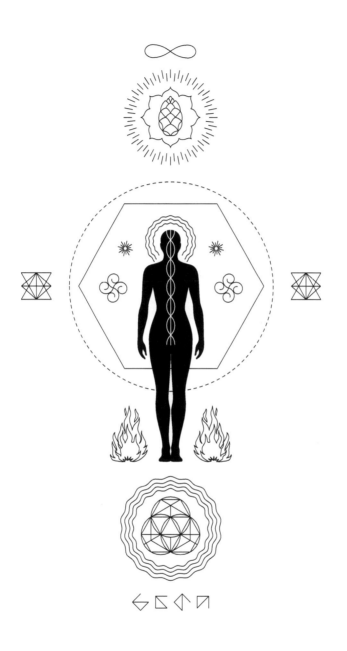

WE ARE A CONDUIT
The Society for The Infinite Spark *of* Being

YOUR PAIN BECAME SO REAL

Your pain became your identity didn't it?
How could it not?
It's all you've ever known.

You identify so closely with your pain and your trauma
that the thought of letting go of it scares you.

After all, who would you been then?

It's so comfortable to hurt. It's so familiar to be sad.
It's what you've always done.
You know what to do with sad and you know how to feel depression.
You know how to want and complain, and you know how to be ungrateful.
You know so well how to harbor regret and contempt.
It's gratitude and happiness that you have trouble with isn't it?
You aren't sure how to let it slip away are you?

If you do that who will you be then?
You don't know that person.
That person that isn't weighted down by childhood trauma.

You cuddle it. Wrap yourself in it. Wear it like a hat.
Or maybe a shawl?
This way everyone knows how hard it is for you.
You had it the worst.
Maybe you keep it in your pocket?
Maybe you hide it away in a box,
and only take it out and show it to those closest to you?
That way they know who you are.
They know just how much you hurt.
Maybe you don't show them at all?

Do you hide it from everyone because if you show them
they might tell you it's not the disaster you thought it was?
Maybe you aren't the damaged child you have invested
so much of yourself into being?
Or maybe you know it's just not as real
as you need it to be?

If you're not abused and misunderstood
who would you be then?

REMEMBER YOU ARE MUCH MORE
The Society for The Infinite Spark *of* Being

LOOK UP!

There is a feeling that i get in my chest
when I think of mountains and open spaces.

It's the same feeling I get
when I look up at the thin, wisping, delicate clouds
of an autumn sky.

Or when I look out onto the pink and yellow glow of a
resting sun as is lies down on a watery horizon and melts into twilight.

It's a feeling of carefree elation that resembles the freedom after
a hard, happy cry.

It is the feeling that,
I have been here before and I will return.

It is not my body that speaks
but it is my soul.

It is like I am recalling a time when I was not bound by the body.

When the plains of consciousness were open doors that I would
walk through like rooms in a never ending house.

KNOWING YOU KNOW
WITHOUT KNOWING YOU KNOW
The Society for The Infinite Spark *of* Being

THERE ARE VISIONS

"What are these voices I hear
deep within the loudest silences?"

"Thought forms
bleeding through the veils."

William James was right.

"What are these things I see
during these moments of deafening quiet?"

"These are the other plains. Living at once."

"Are there lessons
in these visions?"

"Though they may be profound
they mean nothing."

"They are all just something else to let go of
aren't they?"

"Do you remember dreaming?
Do you remember how real it all felt?
How your heart raced and pounded."

"I woke up into a dream didn't I?"

"You did."

THEY WILL PROP YOU UP ALONG THE PATH
The Society for The Infinite Spark *of* Being

WHO ARE THEY?

It's not coming out of a vacuum, you know.

Do not ignore these messages.

You'll know when they are real
and you will know when they are not
once you quiet down.

Thought forms that you've never known.
Things that you couldn't possibly
have witnessed in this "waking" reality.
Names you can't recall yet feel drawn to.

Some are trails left by our past.
Others are cracks in the veil
giving us a glimpse into other realms.

We've learned to ignore these calls from beyond.

We've been acculturated into trusting
only that which can be detected by the 5 faulty
senses and quantified by instruments that
were created to be read by these 5 faulty senses.

Trust your heart.

Get quiet and let it open.
Get honest with yourself and be fearless.

Who are they to say?

Let them catch up
with you.

THE MESSENGERS GATHER
The Society for The Infinite Spark *of* Being

A SHIVER

A shiver...
and then light.

Moving up my spine
it draws everything through
the top of my head.

My hands pulled together.
My neck rolls back and the sounds come
tumbling out of my mouth.

I lay face down
prostrate, hands out.

Moving to accommodate the
flow of energy clawing it's way
up to my crown.

I can't see you.
I can only feel you mother.

To know through experience
is the truth.
The rest are just stories meant only to
increase our longing for liberation.

The death of the ego is frightening.
    To see through your identity is frightening.
        To see others as machines working out
            their karma is frightening.

But then upon dropping back
"down" into this plain
you work your curriculum.

REMEMBER THE INCARNATION
The Society for The Infinite Spark *of* Being

THE SOUTH EASTERN COAST AWAKENS

My first recollection of God was at age 15 I believe.
Though my vocabulary was narrow it did not allow for any other name
but God.
It was early morning.
It was fall.
I sat off the coast.
I remember it clearly.

The blue waters of the south eastern coast of the state
are flawless and conducive to spiritual experiences.

I remember sitting quietly alone
when a warm feeling fell over me.

"I am not alone."

I felt surrounded by something.
It didn't come from any one particular direction.

I felt enveloped by it.

At the time I took this as confirmation that
there was a God, and that he was with me.

Over time as my mind grew
and my vocabulary expanded
I recognized this as a feeling of unity with All.

It was a confirmation that I am in fact the ocean
and everything within and without.

Part and parcel.

You can call that what you want.
You can even say that it is God.
But I can say that I am God.
We are so close to god that, like Hanuman,
we are the breath of God.

So breathe
and breathe deep
and know that
"I am."

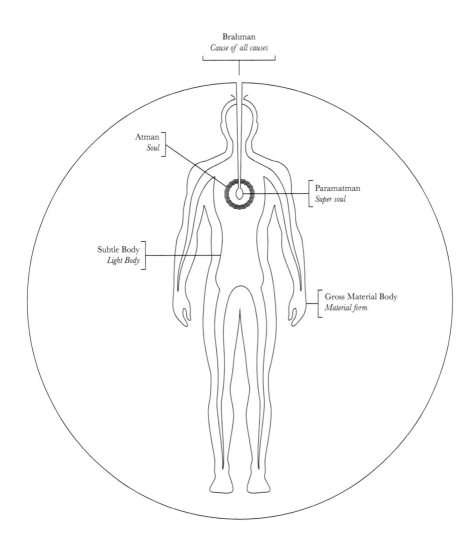

Brahman
Cause of all causes

Atman
Soul

Paramatman
Super soul

Subtle Body
Light Body

Gross Material Body
Material form

ANATOMY OF BEING
The Society for The Infinite Spark *of* Being

THESE MESSENGERS

Some were geometry.
Some like lanterns floating
and lighting my way.
Others tried to speak but I couldn't hear
what they were saying.

These messengers keep a fire lit
that propels our temple toward awakening.

AT TIMES THERE IS A MEETING
The Society for The Infinite Spark *of* Being

AND HERE WE ARE

Well here we are.

You wouldn't believe
what I've been through.

It was like trying to wear shoes
that didn't fit.

But I found you.

You should have seen me
going from face to face
looking into each set of eyes
waiting for you to stare back at me.

AS THE REAL WORK BEGINS
The Society for The Infinite Spark *of* Being

TEARS LIKE NECTAR

If you can't live without the gossip
and drama of consumerism then
what makes you think that you are ready
for the "real" truth?

The bone rattling truth.

That truth that scares you
and shows you your fragility
and your infinite nature all at once.

That truth that changes you
form the inside.

Because no matter what you call the Truth
it will crush you.

It will break you
and terrify you when it shows you
that you are nothing.

Then comes the love.
The holding.
The compassion.

You'll see.

You will cry and you will weep.

And those tears will not be, as they say,
the urine that pours from your eyes over loss.

Those tears of devotion will be purposeful.
They will be what teachers have called "nectar".

And as Ajahn Chah said,
"If you haven't wept deeply,
you haven't begun to meditate."

ONCE I OPENED MY EYES
The Society for The Infinite Spark *of* Being

THEY LIED TO YOU

They lied to you.

You are not this body.
You are in fact a part of every single thing in this universe.

You are the cosmos.
You gave birth to the stars.

Now if you only knew how infinite you are.

One day you will drop this body and live on,
and at that time this will all just be a dream you once had.

YOU ARE A PART OF EVERY SINGLE
THING IN THE UNIVERSE
The Society for The Infinite Spark *of* Being

WATER AND RAIN

In this dream I was a songwriter and an artist.
I fell madly in love with you.

Do you remember how hard it was?
What we went through to find one another?

I am always so reluctant to do this over and over again.
There is always that fear that I won't find you.

Though I always trust the process,
still there are powerful illusions in this world.
But none could keep me from you.

At times I feel like I dug through stone with my bare hands to find you.
Other times I laugh at how perfect it all is, and at the worry
that I may never lay eyes on you again.

How foolish.

You can't separate water from rain.

GOD IS RELATIVE
The Society for The Infinite Spark *of* Being

STAY IN LOVE WITH ALL OF IT

Cry.
It's ok.

It hurts right now I know.
Let it.

Let the pain sit with you.

Feel into your body.

A broken heart is felt in the body.
Hurt feelings are felt in the body.
A shattered sense of identity is felt in the body.

So go to that part of your body
and be with it.

Close your eyes,
put your arms around your broken heart
and cry.

Then realize that you are not that.

Let the tears well up and
slide down those bright red cheeks.
And again realize, that you are not that.

When the grief has run its course
it will let you know.
And at that point you let it fall away.

Let it slip into the clear white light
with the rest of your lessons learned.

Part ways with the pain
right then and there but
stay in love with all of it.

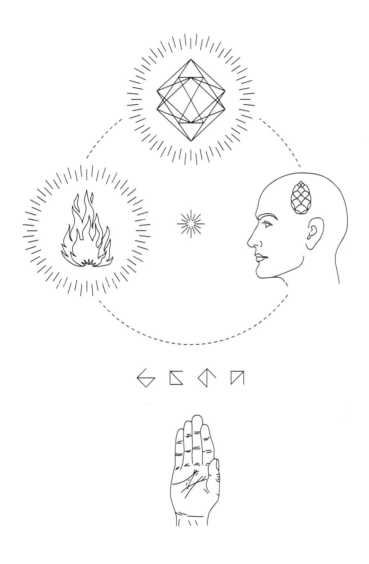

GOING TOWARD THE SUFFERING
The Society for The Infinite Spark *of* Being

I SAW THROUGH THE VEIL TODAY

I saw through the veil today.

It was made of tiny pieces
that looked like dimly lit stars.

That feeling stayed with me
for several hours.

I was seeing all of this as it is.
Tiny pieces held together.

I drove through intersections.
Seeing everything slow and deliberate.
It no longer looked like chaos to me.
It was all functioning as it should.

The perfection was unnoticeable
in the moment as it just felt proper
and true.

Slowly though the veil closed
and rather than being left with
an auspicious vision
and a feeling of peace,
I was right back where I started.

I am a Gemini.
I am a white male.
I am 40 years old,
and I live in America.

We can only visit.

We cannot stay there.

Our work is here
on this plain.

THE MECHANICS OF UNDERSTANDING
The Society for The Infinite Spark *of* Being

I WAS GLOWING

There were mountains.
I remember so vividly.
These valleys that were green.

I flew over them.

I could see straight down,
to the tops of the trees.

They brought me to tunnels of light
where angels lead me.

At least I thought they were angels.

They were white.
They were glowing bright like stars racing through
pathways.

Even I was glowing.

They knew me.
They knew everything about me.
They had no faces that I could see,
but I felt like they were smiling.
They felt childish and wise.

I could cry. If I push I will cry.

I can feel the light
on my fingers even now.

Elation rises in my throat
when I think of these things.

There are other dimensions
made of love.
There are bright glowing halls.
Pathways leading to other realms
where love is unrecognizable as love
because it is all there is.

You will go,
and you will forget.
We all do.
It's part of our way.
To be thoughtless.
To simply pass through beauty,
and leave it behind.

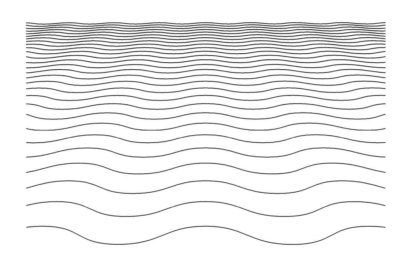

HOW INFINITE YOU ARE
The Society for The Infinite Spark *of* Being

YOU WERE ONCE IN LOVE

Some days are spent quiet.
Staying within that contemplative state
that I can only visit.

This world awakens my ego
and rattles my bones.
It drives its nails through the hearts
of those brave enough to stare
at its short comings.
Brave enough to see it as it is.

Don't run from those fires Sister.
Let your heart burn.
Sit in the places you fear the most.
You are more brave than you know,
and stronger than you care to admit.

There are no accidents.
The lessons maybe be harsh,
and who am I to say, but could this
pain be another strike of the blacksmith's hammer?
Forging the blade you will use next time to slice through
to the center that you may rediscover your Self in time.

Don't close your eyes Brothers.
Stare straight into the suffering.
Find the softness and love in those you understand the least.
They were once children loved by someone that wanted
the best for them, and at one point you loved them too.
We have all been everything to one another,
but we forgot how to love.
We forgot how to see clearly.

Open your heart.
Know that you are That.
Know that they are That.
There is no other.
Yes it is fun to play in duality, but please
when you play rough with one another never forget
that you were once in love.

FIND YOUR WAY BACK AND DO THIS AGAIN
The Society for The Infinite Spark *of* Being

WE GO ON FOREVER

We were under a tree
on the side of a hill.

The sun is bright here.
Everything is lit
with golden light.

We wear white and laugh.
We rest on blankets against hillsides
where the wind rolls down into
valleys and fields.

When I am aware of these places
it's like looking through a veil
into a world that I remember.

In these places my vision is
always consumed with light.
The grass is the brightest green
and it goes on forever.

We go on forever.

These places exist along side us.
Sometimes the veil gets thin, and
other times it parts completely.

It's like going home.

There is an elation in my throat
that rushes into my chest.
I feel home sick for these places
and hopeful that I will return one day.

I miss you.
All of you.

AS WE BEGIN OUR EXPANSION
The Society for The Infinite Spark *of* Being

IF I COULD WORSHIP YOU

I would go there during that golden hour.
There was a bench along that trail.
The sun would turn the leaves a golden green.
I would sit and bask in the still and biting air.
Where decisions to leave and
float south were made.
Promises were made to myself
and whatever god would listen.
Mantras mumbled.
Beads rolling fast in my fingers.

I took you there.

It was like coming full circle.
Like finally finding a shoreline
after so many years at sea.

If I could worship you I would.
If there was a mantra that praised you
I would recite it constantly.

You brought me back.

I was wondering drunk in the dark.

"The path is gone and I can't find my way home."

You lit lanterns.
Not for me, but for yourself.
I followed your light till we were side by side.
Fingers intertwined.

I will never let go into the dark again.
I promise.

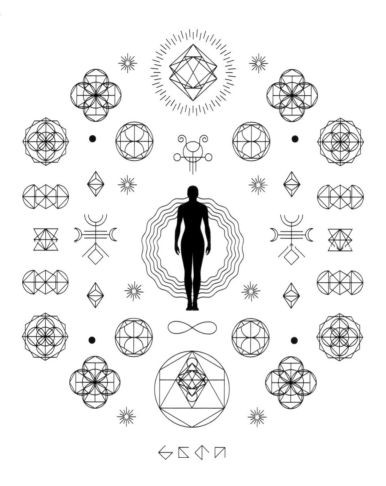

FROM NOW ON
The Society for The Infinite Spark *of* Being

Made in the USA
Middletown, DE
21 April 2021